Hush Hush, Forest

Mary Casanova

Woodcuts by Nick Wroblewski

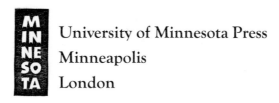

University of Minnesota Press
Minneapolis
London

Published by the University of Minnesota Press
111 Third Avenue South, Suite 290
Minneapolis, MN 55401-2520
http://www.upress.umn.edu

Library of Congress Cataloging-in-Publication Data
Casanova, Mary, author. | Wroblewski, Nick, illustrator.
Hush hush, forest / Mary Casanova ; woodcuts by Nick Wroblewski.
Minneapolis : University of Minnesota Press, [2018]
Summary: Illustrations and easy-to-read, rhyming text show how, throughout autumn, forest animals prepare for
    winter as shadows lengthen, the ground freezes, and northern lights begin to appear.
Identifiers: LCCN 2017057977 | ISBN 978-0-8166-9425-9 (hc/j)
Subjects: | CYAC: Stories in rhyme. | Forest animals–Fiction. | Forests and forestry–Fiction. | Autumn–Fiction.
Classification: LCC PZ8.3.C267 Hus 2018 | DDC [E]–dc23
LC record available at https://lccn.loc.gov/2017057977

Printed in China on acid-free paper

The University of Minnesota is an equal-opportunity educator and employer.

26 25 24 23 22   10 9 8 7 6 5 4 3

For Olivia, and for her parents, who love her
                        —M. C.

Mother, for tending the fire.
Wife, for affording me the time.
Daughter, so marvelous, no woodcut rivals.
                        —N. W.

As we
read our
bedtime
stories,

blankets
tucked
beneath
your chin,

golden leaves

twirl past

our windows,

shadows lengthen,

fall sets in.

Speckled stars
   on agile diver,
      loon sings one last lullaby,

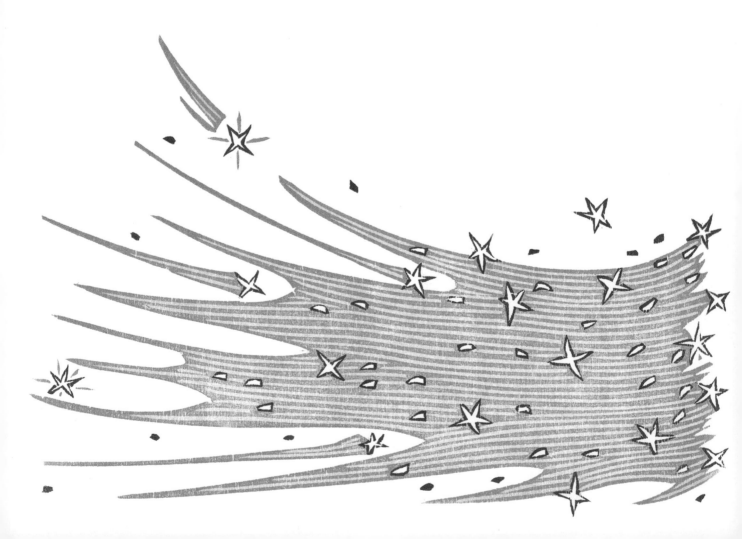

WOO-AHH-WOO-WOO-WOO . . .

to the sky.

rising

rising

Sharp teeth,
strong jaws,

beaver builds a cozy lodge.

Soon the aspen leans

and . . .

DROPS!

Sturdy branches,
leafy tops.

Darting,

zipping

hummingbird,

whirring wings   and ruby
throat,

one last sip

then off he flies,

to warmer breezes,

sunny skies.

Bandit mask
and stealthy paws,
raccoon gobbles crayfish claws.

Waist grows fat and pelt grows thick.

WASH AND PREEN,
WHISKERS CLEAN!

Doe and fawn
 bed down in dry leaves,

  sheltered from
   a bitter wind.

Buck tests his strength against a trunk,

then rubs a scrape
to prove he won.

Wings unfurled,
bat swoops and sweeps,
but no mosquitoes can be found.

She flits to find her colony
and roosts above the
frozen ground.

Northern lights
like wisps of fire,

FLASH and FLARE across the sky.

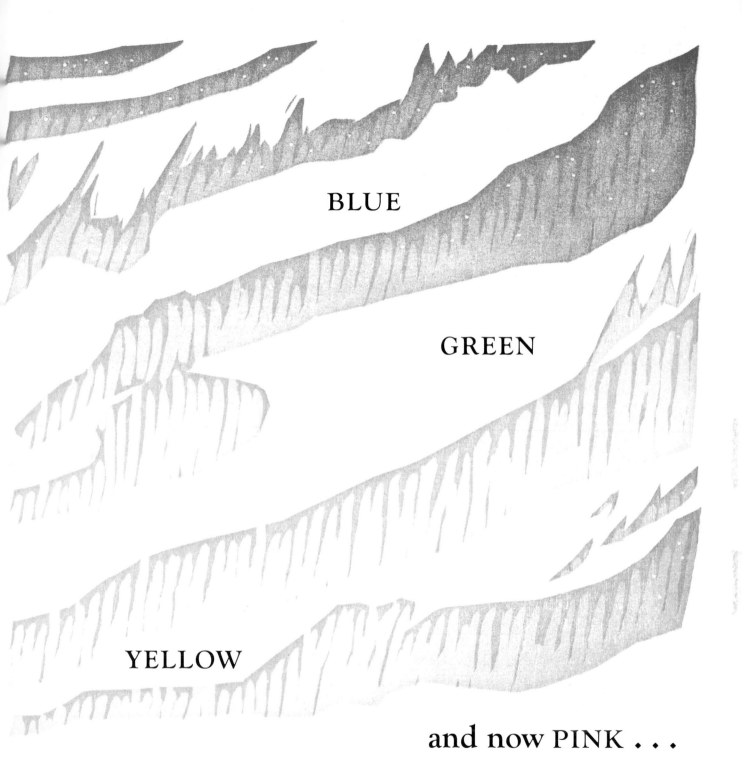

BLUE

GREEN

YELLOW

and now PINK . . .

flicker,
dance,
and mystify.

Owl surveys

from edge of cedars,

eyes glow bright

as moon's cold beam.

Wings stretch wide,

she dips and glides.

Rabbit scurries.

Rabbit hides.

Bear stands huffing,

snorting, warning,

popping jaws 'til coast is clear.

Calls down cubs.
It's time to den.

With gentle paws
she draws them in.

As you close
your eyes
in slumber,

snowflakes slowly
drift and spin.

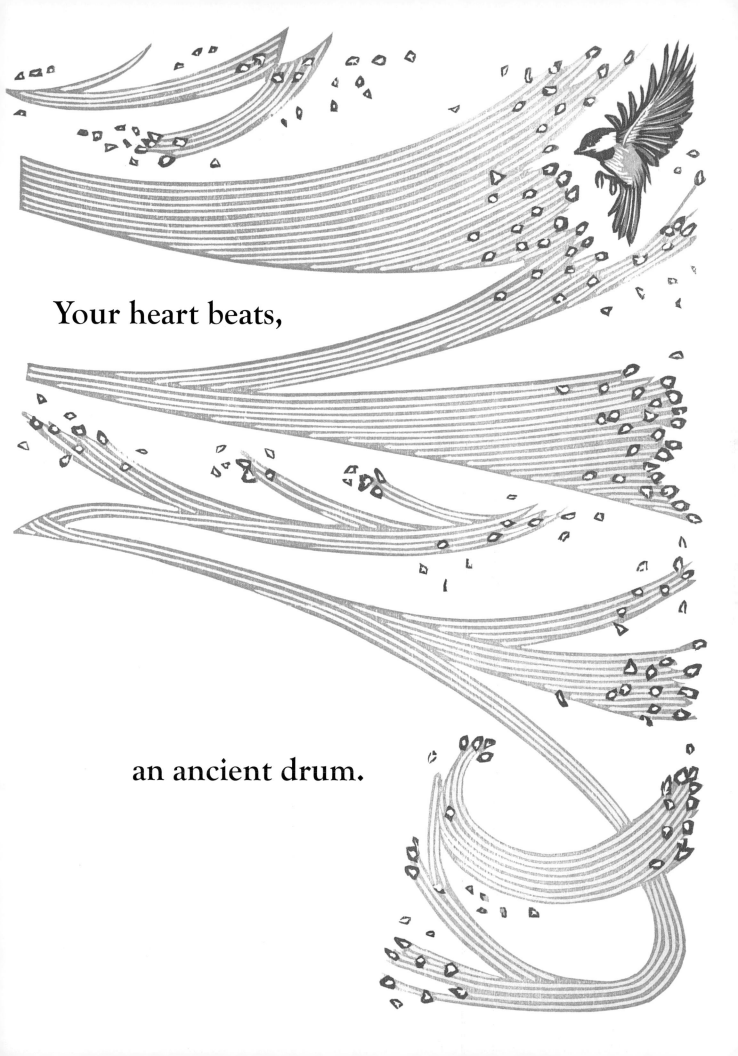

Your heart beats,

an ancient drum.

Hush
hush,
forest,

winter's come.

Mary Casanova is the author of dozens of award-winning books for readers of all ages, ranging from picture books such as *Wake Up, Island* (Minnesota, 2016), which was awarded a National Outdoor Book Award Honorable Mention, to novels, including *Frozen* and *Ice-Out* (Minnesota, 2012, 2016). Her books are on many reading lists and have received two Minnesota Book Awards, the American Library Association Notable Award, Aesop Accolades from the American Folklore Society, Parents' Choice Gold Award, and Booklist Editors' Choice. She speaks frequently around the country at schools and libraries and lives in Minnesota near the Canadian border.

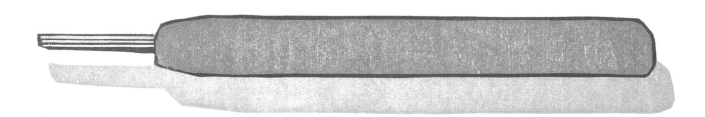

Nick Wroblewski is an artist and printmaker specializing in handmade woodcut blockprints; his art is in private collections and galleries throughout the country. He illustrated Mary Casanova's book *Wake Up, Island* (Minnesota, 2016) and lives in Duluth, Minnesota, with his wife and two children. His prints can be found at www.nickwroblewski.com.